Parasites & Partners

FEEDERS

Rob Houston

First published 2003 by Raintree, a division of Reed Elsevier Inc.
© 2003 The Brown Reference Group plc

Library of Congress Cataloging-in-Publication Data

Houston, Rob.
 Feeders / Rob Houston.
   p. cm. — (Parasites and partners)
Summary: A comprehensive look at different types of parasites that feed
on the blood, dead skin cells, or other parts of host animals, generally
without causing injury.
Includes bibliographical references and index.
 ISBN 0-7398-6988-4 (lib. bdg.) — ISBN 1-4109-0355-9 (pbk.)
 1. Parasites—Juvenile literature. [1. Parasites.] I. Title. II.
Series.
 QL757.H68 2004
 591.7'857—dc21

                    2003004220

ISBN 0-7398-6988-4

Printed and bound in Singapore.
1 2 3 4 5 6 7 8 9 0 07 06 05 04 03 02

Acknowledgements

The publisher would like to thank the following for permission to use photographs:

Key: l – left, r – right, c – center, t – top, b – bottom.
Ardea: Brian Bevan 13b, Ferrero-Labat 23, Francois Gohier 29t, Clem Haagner 27t, Steve Hopkin 24t, P. Morris 9t, 12b, A. Warren
7; **Bruce Coleman Collection:** John Cancalosi 24b; **Corbis:** Nigel Dennis/Gallo Images 27b, Joe McDonald 29b; **Jeff Jeffords:** 4ct;
Natural Science Photos: Mary Clay 28t, N. K. D. Miller 20–21; **Nature Picture Library:** Jose B. Ruiz 20, Sinclair Stammers 15;
NHPA: Laurie Campbell 8b, Daniel Heuclin 18t; **Oceanic Impressions/Mark Strickland:** 13t; **Oxford Scientific Films:** 21; **PHIL:** 4b,
18b, CDC/Janice Carr 4cb, James Gathany 11b; **Photodisc:** Frank & Joyce Burek 26; **Dr. Hans Pohl:** 5b, 19; **Science Photo Library:**
James King-Holmes 16, David Scharf 17b, Sinclair Stammers 17t; **Still Pictures:** John Cancalosi 5t; **USDA/ARS:** 10, Scott Bauer 11t,
Ray Carruthers 5c, Jack Dykinga 4t, Eric Erbe & Chris Pooley 8t, 30
Front Cover: ARS/USDA: Eric Erbe & Chris Pooley (t); **PHIL:** James Gathany (b)

For The Brown Reference Group

Project Editor: Jim Martin
Consultancy Board: Dr. Kimberley N. Russell, Division of
   Invertebrate Zoology, American Museum of Natural
   History, New York; Prof. Marilyn Scott, Institute of
   Parasitology, McGill University, Montreal, Canada
Designed by: Pewter Design Associates
Illustrator: Mike Woods
Picture Researcher: Helen Simm
Managing Editor: Bridget Giles
Art Director: Dave Goodman
Production Director: Alastair Gourlay

Raintree

Editor: Jim Schneider
Managing Editor: Jamie West
Production Manager: Brian Suderski

Front cover: A straw itch mite on a caterpillar (*top*);
a mosquito feeds from a human finger (*bottom*).

Title page: This sea slug bears pockets on its body that
contain chloroplasts. These provide sugars to the animal.

Note to the Reader
Some words are shown in bold, like **this.** You can find out what they mean by looking in "Words to Know."

Parasites & Partners
FEEDERS

Contents

Introduction

Animals and plants do not live alone. They are always interacting with other creatures. A close association between different species is called a **symbiosis.** *Parasites & Partners* introduces you to symbiotic relationships. You can see examples of these around you every day. Anyone who keeps a dog shares a symbiosis with their pet. The dog is fed and housed by its owner, who gains a companion and protection in return. Both partners in this relationship benefit, but that is not always the case. The different types of symbioses covered in this book are discussed in the box below.

Each book in *Parasites & Partners* looks at a different group of relationships. Find out how plants and animals interact with other types of creatures as they feed, breed, keep clean, find a home, and move around.

4

Some important words for you to remember

Mutualism
Biologists call a relationship in which both partners benefit a **mutualism.** In this example, the bee is taking nectar from the flower back to its nest, while the plant is using the bee to spread its pollen to other flowers.

Commensalism
A relationship in which one **organism** benefits but the other neither profits nor suffers is called a **commensalism.** The unaffected partner is usually called the **host.** Here, a crinoid shrimp blends with the colors of its feather star host.

Ectoparasite
A creature that benefits at the expense of another and lives on or visits its skin or outer surface is called an **ectoparasite.** The organisms they attack are called hosts. This flea lives on the body of a rat and feeds on its blood.

Endoparasite
An organism that benefits at the expense of another and lives inside its body is called an **endoparasite.** Again, the creatures they attack are called hosts. This is a nematode worm. It lives inside the wall of a person's gut.

◄ *To break down food, koalas need the help of tiny creatures in their guts. Learn more about feeding partnerships on pages 22–29.*

▼ *A leech inches forward in search of a warm-blooded victim. Discover bizarre bloodsuckers and skin munchers on pages 6–13.*

5

In **this** book...

...you will learn how creatures interact with each other in the search for food. Many animals and plants are **parasites** that live on their hosts or visit from time to time. In chapter one, we look at these skin munchers and bloodsuckers. In chapter two, find out about parasites that have an even closer relationship with their hosts. These parasites live inside their hosts, in the bloodstream, gut, or tissues.

Not all feeding relationships involve parasites. In the final chapter, discover creatures that work with others as a team for food. In these cases both partners benefit. We also learn about animals that rely on other creatures for food without affecting their providers.

▼ *This twisted-winged parasite grew up inside the body of another insect before bursting free. Find out more about parasites that live inside their hosts on pages 14–21.*

Drinking **BLOOD** and Eating **SKIN**

6

Many animals live as parasites on the bodies of other animals. Some feed on flakes of dead skin, fur, or feathers, while others pierce the skin and drink the host's blood. Many other blood drinkers visit the host to feed but do not live there permanently.

When a **parasite** feeds, it eats small pieces of its victim. It never eats a whole animal or a whole plant. Most parasites eat so little that the **host** hardly notices. A parasite can live on or inside its host for a long time, often for its entire life. Many parasites live on the outside of their hosts. These are called **ectoparasites.**

Eating out

Hosts produce lots of tasty substances on their body surfaces that ectoparasites can eat. For example, birds and mammals constantly shed flakes of dead skin. They also ooze oily liquids that keep their skin, fur, or feathers in good condition.

Tiny relatives of spiders and scorpions called mites and small, flat insects called lice

▲ A vampire bat laps at a puddle of blood on the skin of a sleeping donkey.

There are skin munchers in the oceans, too. Just as land animals shed flakes of skin and produce oils, fish shed scales and produce protective **mucus**. Again, there are ectoparasites that come to dine, called sea lice. Sea lice are not insects like the lice on mammals and birds. They are crustaceans—distant cousins of shrimps, crabs, and lobsters.

Harmless parasites

Some ectoparasites are virtually harmless to their hosts. For example, follicle mites live on hairy animals, including people. On people, follicle mites like living on faces, in beards, and even within the roots of eyelashes. They hide inside follicles, which are holes in the skin where hair roots are buried.

Follicle mites exploit a strange food source. They sip tiny amounts of the oil produced by skin to keep hairs from drying out. The skin might make a little extra oil to make up for the loss, but the effect of the mites is far too tiny for a human host to notice.

crawl around feeding on the oils and flakes of skin. Mites can be very tiny. Five of the smallest could fit on the period at the end of this sentence. Lice are not much bigger. Most are smaller than a pinhead.

▲ *This straw itch mite has made its home on the skin of a butterfly caterpillar.*

8

◀ *Sea lice gather by a wound on a fish. These parasites feed on scales and drink blood if they get the chance.*

Lovely lice

Insects such as lice that live on the bodies of other animals look very different from other insects. Lice never leave their hosts, so they have no need to fly and are wingless. Eyesight is of little use under a coat of fur, and lice can find their way around with tiny eyes or none at all. Lice have flat bodies with short legs and feelers. This helps them clamber through dense forests of fur or feathers. Many other ectoparasitic insects have features like these. Batflies, for example, are only distantly related to lice, but the two groups are hard to tell apart.

Lice can live in very odd places. Curlew quill lice live inside the shafts of a curlew's flight feathers, while pelican lice live

▶ *Squat, wingless, and with tiny eyes, this batfly looks more like a louse than a fly.*

▼ *Mites can cause serious problems for a male damselfly. Female damselflies prefer to mate with mite-free males.*

9

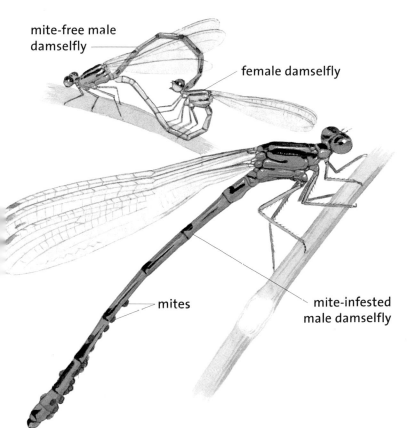

mite-free male damselfly

female damselfly

mites

mite-infested male damselfly

inside a pelican's pouch. These lice climb through the nostrils of their hosts to lay eggs on the head feathers.

Hiding out

Fur and feathers provide a lot of places for tiny parasites to hide. Birds and mammals also produce plenty of body heat. The warmth protects parasites from frost and allows them to grow quickly. With warmth and a steady supply of food, the skin of birds and mammals make good homes for parasites. Some parasites even use hairs or feathers for food. Thousands of species of biting lice live on this tough diet.

Sap suckers

Just like animals, plants have parasite food flowing through their veins. This is sap, a liquid full of sugars that flows around the plant. Many insects with piercing and sucking mouthparts tap into this rich food resource.

Aphids are sap-sucking insects. Like sucking lice, aphids spend their entire lives on their hosts. They tap into plant veins, drawing the sweet liquid through their mouthparts. Unlike blood, sap does not contain all the nutrients an animal needs. It has lots of water and sugars but not many proteins or fats. An aphid must suck a lot of sap to get enough proteins and fats, but it gets far more sugar and water than it needs. The aphid passes most of the sugar straight out of its rear end as a sticky liquid called honeydew. At the height of summer in a maple forest, honeydew from millions of aphids rains down from the canopy.

▲ *Peach aphids plug into a leaf.*

Not all ectoparasites are as harmless as biting lice. Mange mites burrow little tunnels into the bodies of animals such as sheep and dogs. The mites glue eggs to the tunnel walls and feed on bits of skin. The mites cause such itchy irritation that the host scratches. The skin reacts by forming weeping scabs. This makes more food for the mange mites, which enjoy the scabby dead skin and body fluids, but it is itchy torment for the host.

A taste for blood

Just beneath the host's skin flows a red river of food much richer and more nutritious than dead skin or fur. Blood carries food and oxygen around the host's body to tissues and organs. The blood also provides food for a lot of sneaky parasites. Although blood flows through **blood vessels** buried in a host's body, parasites can get at it from all directions, inside and out.

In places, blood vessels run very close to the surface and within reach of ectoparasites that have the right mouthparts. Most blood-drinking parasites have piercing, sucking mouthparts. Sucking lice, for example, have a set of long, pointed mouthparts. There is a central prong called a proboscis. Surrounding this are three sharp, hollow mouthparts called stylets. The sucking louse pierces the host's skin with its proboscis. The stylets then plunge into a blood vessel near the surface. The louse sucks blood through the stylets.

Other sucking creatures

Many other small animals use piercing and sucking mouthparts to drink blood. Most are not as devoted to their host as lice are, though. Some, such as ticks, blackflies, and mosquitoes, only visit the host to feed. Adult mosquitoes usually feed on flower **nectar.** Nectar provides energy, but it does not contain all the nutrients that a female mosquito needs to make her eggs. She gets these by stealing a wholesome meal of blood.

It is not just mammals and birds that are the victims of insect bloodsuckers. Some midges feed on other insects. They drink liquid from the wing veins of insects such as dragonflies and lacewings. A few midges even steal human blood from well-fed mosquitoes.

Night stalkers

Mammals are often targets for bloodsucking insects, but did you know that there is a group of mammals that likes to drink blood, too? These are called vampire bats. Feared and famous, these bats live in South and Central America. They rarely drink human blood, but they

▲ *This is a cattle tick. When ticks feed, they take in a lot of blood and swell to many times their original size. Some ticks can go for three years after such a meal!*

11

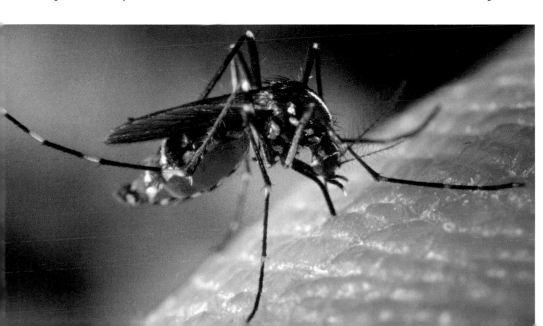

◀ *Her body red with human blood, a female mosquito prepares to make a speedy getaway from her host.*

Cheaters never prosper

Life can be tough for a vampire bat. It needs to feed every night, otherwise it may starve. However, vampire bats cope with short-term food shortages in a remarkable way.

A bat that has failed to find a victim will beg for food from a more successful bat. The well-fed bat passes over some of its blood meal, but only if it knows that its hungry friend can be trusted to return the favor.

Vampire bats are able to recognize individual bats as friends or foes. Some bats try to cheat the system. They take food when they are hungry but do not give blood in return at a later date. Cheating bats lose the trust of their roostmates, and are more likely to die when food is in short supply.

▲ *A vampire bat shares its meal.*

often attack horses, cattle, and chickens. Vampire bats use their razor-sharp front teeth to cut a little hole in their victim's skin, often around the ankles. The bats lap up the blood that flows from the wound. Like many blood feeders, vampire bats have a chemical in their saliva that stops the host's blood from forming a scab. This allows the blood to flow freely until the bat is full.

Underwater vampires

Many bloodsucking animals live in the ocean. Lampreys are fish that can live in both salty and fresh waters. The young feed by trailing strands of mucus in the current to catch small animals. Adult lampreys feed in a different

▼ *A lamprey prepares to strike out at a passing fish. The lamprey will use its rows of teeth to gouge a hole in the body of its victim.*

way. They do not have jaws but a round sucker filled with rows of sharp teeth and a rough, scratchy tongue. An adult lamprey ambushes other fish. It clamps its mouth onto the host's body. Then it uses its teeth and tongue to tear a hole through the host's skin. The lamprey then drinks blood and other body fluids.

Perhaps the strangest of the underwater bloodsuckers is the vampire snail. Vampire snails are far too slow to launch an ambush on a fast-moving fish, so they use stealth instead.

At night, the snail trundles slowly across a coral reef in search of a host. When the snail finds a sleeping fish, it crawls onto its body. The snail extends its sharp proboscis and drills a small hole in the fish's skin. Then the snail sucks up a meal of tasty fish blood.

Lurking leeches

Leeches are famous for their bloodsucking abilities. They need plenty of moisture, so most lurk in ponds or slow-moving rivers. Some rain forest leeches, though, live on damp leaves and branches.

▲ *A vampire snail crawls over the mucus cocoon of a sleeping parrot fish and uses its long proboscis to drink the fish's blood.*

◄ *Leeches use their powerful suckers to attach themselves securely to the host while they feed.*

Leeches ambush passing animals. A leech uses its sharp mouthparts to cut a neat Y-shaped hole in the animal's skin. The leech then inserts a sucking tube. Chemicals in the leech's saliva keep the blood flowing and also numb the host's flesh. The host feels no pain, so it does not brush the leech off.

Leeches earned their fame because doctors once used them to draw blood from their patients as a cure for sickness. Leeches are still used today when a severed body part, such as a hand, is reattached. The leech sucks blood from the body part until blood begins to flow through naturally.

13

KEY FACTS

■ A bloodsucking cattle tick can swell with blood to become more than 1 inch (2.5 cm) long.

■ To collect leeches from the wild, people poured pig blood into a flooded ditch or pond. The leech

hunters waded into the water with their pants rolled up and collected the leeches on their legs.

■ Over the last 100 years, lampreys have decimated populations of fish in the Great Lakes.

Life **INSIDE**

If a parasite can get inside a host and overcome its defenses, a banquet of food awaits. All the invader then has to do is complete the difficult journey through the host's body to a good feeding spot, and the parasite's food worries are over.

14

Animals that invade a **host** and live inside its body are called **endoparasites.** An endoparasite might live in a host's gut, liver, bloodstream, or even its brain. Wherever it lives, an endoparasite is surrounded by things it can eat. This can be blood, tissues, or the host's food as it travels through the gut.

Despite plentiful food, life is not easy for an endoparasite. The body of another animal can be a hostile place. The host fights endoparasites with **white blood cells.** These move around the body destroying invaders.

Gut parasites

There are few places better for a **parasite** to live than inside an animal's gut. A gut parasite is safe from white blood cells, since blood does not enter the gut. It is also warm, and food passes by as if on a conveyor belt.

Animals **digest** (break down) food in their gut with powerful chemicals called **enzymes.** Digested food is **absorbed** into the animal's blood through its gut walls. This is good news for gut parasites, since they do not need to digest their own food. Their host does that job for them.

◄ These nematode worms have recently been removed from the stomach of a dog.

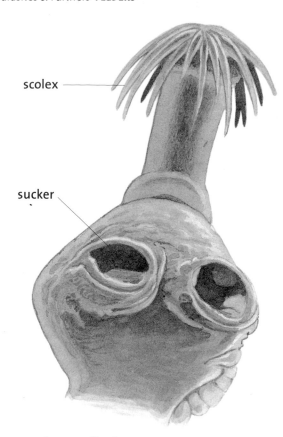

scolex

sucker

Flats, flukes, and tapes

Many endoparasites are types of flatworms, which are a large group of long, thin creatures. Both tapeworms and flukes are types of flatworms.

Tapeworms are superbly suited to living in the guts of other animals. They lie in their host's gut, bathed in food. So, they have no need for eyes, other sense organs, or even a gut of their own. Instead, tapeworms absorb the host's digested food through their skin. Tapeworms have a flat, narrow shape that provides a large surface area over which to absorb food. Animal guts are coiled and very long, and tapeworms can reach giant lengths, too. Human tapeworms can reach

◀ *The head of a tapeworm. The scolex acts like an anchor. It is buried deep in the wall of the host's gut to keep the worm in place. Suckers provide further grip.*

▼ *Some tapeworms are enormous. This one, taken from a sheep's gut, measures nearly 20 feet (6 m) long!*

36 feet (9 m) long, while whale tapeworms can be measure up to 100 feet (30 m) long!

A tapeworm can draw in all the nutrients it needs, but it must be choosy about where in the gut it lives. It can only absorb food that has been fully broken down. Food gets broken down more and more as it travels along an animal's gut. A tapeworm can stretch its body, though, to ensure it reaches the right kind of food.

Tapeworms and other gut parasites compete with their hosts to absorb nutrients. For example, a tapeworm has a huge appetite for vitamin B12, which it needs to produce millions of eggs. Tapeworms usually beat their host in the competition for this vitamin. A lack of vitamin B12 in the host causes disorders of the blood, brain, and nerves.

Lucky fluke

The parasite with the highest-quality diet could be the liver fluke. This flatworm lives in the bile duct. Along this tube, bile travels from inside the liver to the gut, where it helps digest fats. Animals store a lot of nutrients in the liver, so liver cells provide a particularly rich food source for parasites. A liver fluke is surrounded by liver cells. By chewing the walls of the bile duct, it receives a nutritious diet of liver cells and blood.

▶ *This liver fluke lives in a human bile duct.*

Digesting food

Apart from tapeworms, most parasitic worms have their own guts. So, they do not have to rely on their host to break down their food. Gut-living nematodes and many flukes take food in through their mouths and break it down with their own digestive juices.

Some gut parasites ignore the plentiful part-digested food passing by. Instead they dive headfirst into the gut wall to eat the host's tissues and blood. A sheep nematode sucks a lump of gut wall into its huge mouth and begins digesting the sheep's tissues. The worm then pumps the liquid food down its throat to its own gut.

17

Fighting the flow

A big problem for gut parasites is how to avoid being swept away by the river of food. Tapeworms dig their heads into the gut wall. Hookworms have sharp fanglike prongs around their mouths that they sink into the gut wall.

Hookworms belong to a group of worms called nematodes. Most nematodes are threadlike and tiny, but giant nematodes, which live inside people, can grow up to 20 inches (50 cm) long. Giant nematodes do not attach to the gut wall but keep swimming to avoid being swept away. They can even swim up the throat and emerge in someone's mouth!

▶ *The spikes inside this hookworm's mouth help the worm attach to the wall of its host's gut.*

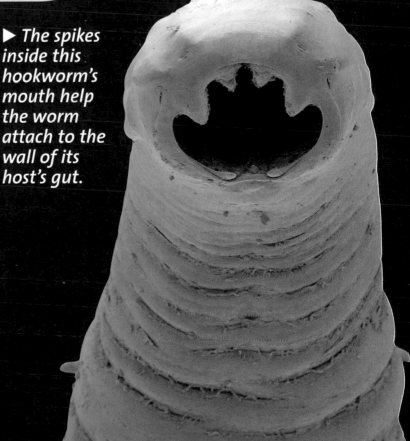

Little dragons

The scientific name of the guinea worm, *Dracunculus*, means "little dragon," and this nematode truly is a fearsome beast. Young guinea worms live inside tiny shrimplike water animals called *Cyclops* in parts of Africa and Asia. People may accidentally swallow a *Cyclops* when they drink. The worms escape from the *Cyclops* as it is digested. They drill their way out of the gut, then travel through the blood to a point just beneath the skin. After mating, a female guinea worm creates a blister in the skin. When the blister comes into contact with water, the worm releases young through it. The young worms then swim off to look for *Cyclops*. People can remove an adult worm through the blister. They tie the end of the worm to a piece of string or wrap it around a stick and gently draw the worm out. This must be done slowly—otherwise the worm may snap in two. Since females can grow to 4 feet (1.2 m) long, the removal process can take weeks.

▶ *A guinea worm is removed.*

18

▼ *A human botfly larva uses the spines on its body to wedge itself into flesh.*

rows of spines

Cells and bloodstream

The gut is not the only part of the host's body that supports endoparasites. Many feed on host tissues or blood. **Blood vessels** are dangerous places for parasites, because the host's white blood cells are constantly on patrol. Tiny parasites such as *Plasmodium*, which causes the disease malaria, hide inside **red blood cells** and eat them from the inside.

Larger blood parasites use tricks to fool host defenses. For example, schistosome worms attach tiny pieces of host material to their body surfaces. Disguised as part of the host, the worms cannot be recognized as enemies by the host's white blood cells.

Schistosomes feed on blood. Once a schistosome has eaten and digested a meal, it has to bring up its waste products through its mouth. It cannot pass waste through its rear end because its gut has only one opening—the mouth.

Bizarre botflies

Many parasites live inside tissues around the body. Botflies are insects that attack a wide range of animals, including people. A human botfly **larva** (young insect) digs through the skin and into muscle tissue. There, it feeds

◀ *This horse botfly has laid her eggs on the legs of a horse. As the horse nibbles the infested hairs, the eggs hatch, and the young burrow into the horse's mouth.*

▼ *A female twisted-wing parasite pokes her rear end out of the host's body. The insect releases chemicals to attract a flying male.*

and grows, remaining connected to the outside world through a narrow breathing tube. After a few months of development, the botfly tunnels out. The insect then drops to the ground, where it changes into an adult.

Some botflies move around the body as they grow. Adult horse botflies lay their eggs on hairs on a horse's legs. The eggs hatch when the horse nibbles at the hairs as it grooms. The larvae burrow into the horse's tongue. There, they develop for about a month before breaking out. The horse swallows the larvae, which live in the horse's stomach for a time before passing through the gut completely. The botflies then change into adults in the soil.

Twisting torment

There are many other insect endoparasites. Twisted-wing parasites are insects that spend at least part of their lives inside other insects such as bees and grasshoppers. Young twisted-wing parasites wait on flower heads before jumping on to a passing insect. They burrow in and drink the insect's blood.

Adult females never leave the host. They have no need for wings or legs, and look just like the larvae. Males, however, do

grow wings. They burst free from the host and fly away in search of females. A female pokes a small part of her body out of the host. This allows the female to mate and provides an exit for her young, which hatch inside her.

Plant parasites

It is not just animals that suffer from endoparasites—plants are attacked, too. The endoparasites of plants can be microorganisms, animals, **fungi,** or even other types of plants. Pale trails can often be found on the leaves of plants. These are tunnels made by the larvae of tiny wasps, moths, and flies. These insects are called leaf miners because they dig burrows through the leaves—just like human miners tunneling through the ground.

▼ These are the flowers of a Maltese fungus plant. The plant sends out shoots to steal sap from the roots of other plants.

20

Parasites live in all parts of plants, not just the leaves. Plant nematodes, for example, live inside the leaves and stems of plants and drink their nutritious, sugary sap. Many plant parasites are plants, too. These parasitic plants extend their stems into the host plant's stem or trunk to draw off water and sap.

The sprigs of mistletoe that people kiss beneath during the holiday season are part of

◄ *Mistletoe plants on an oak tree. Infected trees may wither and die since they lose a lot of sap to the mistletoes.*

a parasitic plant. A mistletoe plant steals food and water from the tree that it lives on.

Most plants are green. The color is produced by a chemical called **chlorophyll.** This chemical traps the energy of sunlight. The plant uses the energy to make sugars that feed the plant. However, many parasitic plants do not have any green color. They have no need for chlorophyll

► *An underground orchid flowers beneath the surface of the soil. The flower will be visited by termites.*

since they steal all their food. One such plant without chlorophyll is called Maltese fungus. It is so strange that people at first did not realize it was a plant. It has no leaves and no true roots. Maltese fungus lives as an underground stem, sending out shoots to steal sap from the roots of other plants.

An Australian parasitic plant called the underground orchid does not even flower above ground. It flowers just below the surface. Termites visit its flowers to collect nectar. The insects carry the plant's pollen to other flowers. This allows the orchids to produce seeds.

21

KEY FACTS

■ The meat of mammals can be riddled with parasites. At least one arctic explorer, for example, has died because of a nematode worm infection caused by eating a poorly cooked polar bear steak.

■ Human botflies mainly attack cattle but also invade the bodies of people.

■ Schistosomes may release sugars into the host's blood to distract its white blood cells.

Working
TOGETHER

In the wild, food is rarely easy to get. Sometimes, different creatures form partnerships that allow both to feed. By working together, they can obtain food that would otherwise be unavailable. Other creatures feed by exploiting the hard work of others.

22

Food is not always easy to **digest** (break down). Juices in an animal's gut contain chemicals called **enzymes.** These chemicals digest the food. Once the food is in small enough pieces, it can be **absorbed** (taken in through the gut wall) into the blood. Some foods are very tough to digest, though. Many animals have microscopic partners that help out.

Plant problems

The leaves and stems of plants are supported by a tough, fibrous material called **cellulose.** People are unable to digest cellulose—it just passes straight through.

An animal that feeds mostly on grass, such as an antelope, eats little else but cellulose. Cellulose contains energy that the antelope needs. To break down cellulose, these animals need help from microorganisms.

▼ Ibis and egrets follow a wandering elephant. The birds feast on insects disturbed by the giant animal's feet.

These are tiny, single-celled creatures such as **protists** that live in the animal's gut. The antelope supplies chewed plant material to protists in its gut. The protists, called ciliates, have the chemical tool kit needed to digest the cellulose. Once the ciliates have taken all the food they need, there are still plenty of nutrients and energy left for the antelope. In return for this digestion, the antelope provides a safe, warm home for the ciliates. Both partners benefit; biologists call this type of relationship a **mutualism.**

Many **organisms** take on a food source that is tougher still to digest—wood. Termites can only break down wood with the help of gut protists called flagellates. The flagellates benefit from a supply of mashed-up, pulpy wood provided by the termite.

▲ Many termites eat wood. They can cause a lot of damage to timbers in buildings as they feed.

The flagellates break the wood down into sugars and fats, which the termite can absorb through its gut wall.

Young animals are not born with their gut helpers. Passing on gut microorganisms to young is a challenge. Like termites, wood roaches need flagellates to break down wood. Young roaches have no flagellates. They take in a drop of liquid from the rear end of one of their parents. The liquid contains the flagellates that the young wood roaches need.

Koalas need microorganisms to digest the tough eucalyptus leaves they eat and to deal with poisons in the leaves. Baby koalas have no microorganisms in their guts when they are born. A koala mother squirts a partly digested green soup of leaves from her rear end. It contains the microorganisms the young koala needs. The youngster might hesitate to eat, but it must swallow the soup.

◄ Koalas eat nothing but eucalyptus leaves. They have tiny creatures in their gut that help them digest this tough diet.

Chemical cooperation

Many organisms team up to exchange essential nutrients. Plants need important nutrients such as nitrogen and phosphorus. To get nitrogen, some plants, especially members of the pea family, team up with tiny **bacteria.** The bacteria take nitrogen gas from the air and turn it into chemicals that the plant needs. The bacteria live in buttons that grow on the pea plant's roots. In exchange for the nitrogen chemicals, the bacteria receive starch and sugars from the pea plant. Neither the pea plant nor the bacteria could survive without the other.

To get phosphorus, plants enter partnerships with **fungi.** Thin plant rootlets merge with a threadlike fungus. The partnership spreads through the soil, forming a mesh of threads that absorbs and exchanges nutrients. The plant roots and fungi are so tightly bound together that they are difficult to tell apart. An entire forest might rely on the fungi entwining roots beneath the surface of the soil.

Solar-powered animals

Although they are animals, corals look a lot like plants. Their colonies often branch like trees, and groups of corals look like thickets of shrubs. Plants and corals are arranged in similar ways because both need to catch as much sunlight as possible. Within the tissues of a coral are tiny organisms called **algae.** The algae use the Sun's energy to make sugars. In return for a safe home inside the coral, the

25

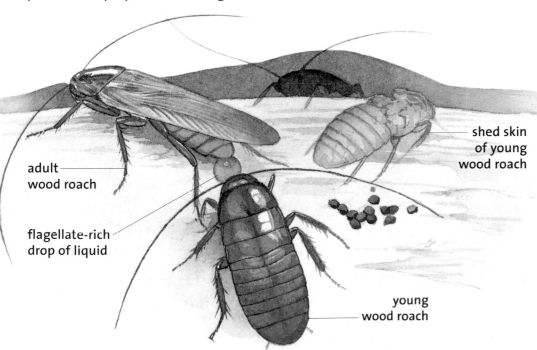

adult
wood roach

flagellate-rich
drop of liquid

shed skin
of young
wood roach

young
wood roach

◀ *Young wood roaches molt their skins to grow. But they also shed their gut lining when they molt, losing their flagellates. They must drink a drop of liquid from the rear end of an adult roach to replace them.*

Taking over food factories

Some types of sea slugs get extra food in a bizarre way. They feed by sucking fluid from algae. However, they do not digest everything they take into their body. The sea slugs preserve the tiny **chloroplasts**. These are little green factories inside the cells of algae and other plantlike organisms. Chloroplasts use energy from the Sun to make sugars for the plant.

The gut of the sea slug branches into a network of fine tubes that spreads throughout its body. The chloroplasts pass to the ends of these tubes. There, they continue making food from sunlight. But rather than delivering food to the algae, they instead provide sugars for the sea slug.

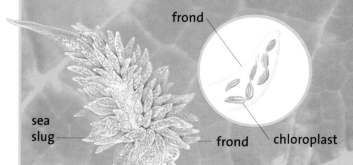

frond

sea
slug

frond   chloroplast

◄ *This sea slug contains chloroplasts in leaflike fronds on its back (inset).*

algae share their sugars with their landlords. The corals use stinging tentacles to catch small animals drifting in the water, but the extra food the algae provides is vital. The waters around coral reefs are not rich with food. There are few tiny floating organisms, which is why the water is so clear. For this reason, many other coral reef animals get help from algae.

▼ *Algae that live in coral tissue provide a vital extra source of food.*

26

eat wax and **larvae** (young insects) from beehives. The birds are good at finding honeybee hives, but they cannot break through the tough walls of the bees' nest.

After finding a hive, a honeyguide searches for a ratel. The bird gives a churring call and flashes its white wing feathers to let the ratel know what it has found. The bird then leads the ratel to the hive. The ratel uses its powerful claws to break into the bees' nest, where it feeds on the honey inside.

Once the ratel has eaten its fill, the bird swoops down to take its share of the spoils. Honeyguides do not just lead ratels to good feeding spots. They also show people where to find a beehive.

27

Many sponges have helpful algae living inside, and so do some jellyfish and sea slugs.

Winning teams

Not all feeding partnerships are with microorganisms such as bacteria and algae. There are many relationships between larger organisms that team up to get food. In Africa, birds called honeyguides form a partnership with an animal called a honey badger, or ratel. Honeyguides love to

▲▼ A ratel (above) and a honeyguide (below) work together for food.

honeycomb

Sniffing and digging

In North America, badgers and coyotes form an effective team to hunt prairie dogs, voles, and ground squirrels. A coyote and a badger wander together in search of food. When they see a squirrel, the coyote gives chase.

If the squirrel dives into its burrow, the badger begins to dig. If the squirrel stays inside, the badger gets a meal, but if the squirrel makes a burst for freedom the coyote pounces. Both coyotes and badgers catch more small mammals when they hunt together than when they hunt on their own.

Something for nothing

Some animals feed by exploiting the work of others. When dolphins hunt small shoals of

▲ *A coyote and a badger team up for food. As the badger digs into a ground squirrel burrow, the coyote waits by the exit.*

fish, for example, large seabirds called gannets follow. The dolphins herd the fish toward the ocean surface to make them easier to catch. Once the fish are near the surface, they are within range of the hungry gannets. The gannets dive like arrows into the water to spear the fish. The birds benefit from the dolphins' skills

KEY FACTS

■ Many mangrove trees have sponges growing on their roots. The sponges pass nitrogen chemicals to the tree and receive sugars in return.

■ Every species of orchid has its own species

of fungus growing around its roots.

■ The lichen that grows on walls and gravestones is actually two creatures living together and sharing food. One is an alga, the other a fungus.

as fish herders, but the dolphins neither suffer nor benefit. Biologists call a relationship like this a **commensalism.**

Easy meals

Commensalisms are very common in nature. Often the movement of animals leads to feeding opportunities for others. A column of army ants disturbs every animal in its path. Antbirds follow the army ants as they march through the forest. Insects fleeing the rampaging ants form an easy meal for the birds.

Many birds enjoy commensal relationships with mammals. Birds such as egrets and storks follow large animals such as elephants, cattle, and buffaloes. As these mammals walk slowly along, they disturb insects in the grass that the birds grab.

A pied cormorant often feeds by keeping close to a very unusual mammal. A duck-billed platypus uses its sensitive snout to search for young insects, shellfish, and worms on the river bottom. The disturbance caused by the platypus sends dirt filled with tiny animals toward the surface. There, the cormorant picks off the tastiest morsels.

▲▼ A pied cormorant (above) will follow a foraging duck-billed platypus (below) and feed from the cloud of dirt it produces.

29

Things to Do

Backyard mite safari

Mites are tiny relatives of spiders. Many live as **ectoparasites** on the bodies of larger animals. Even common animals in your backyard will have a lot of mites. So why not take a backyard mite safari and check out these tiny creatures?

Mites are very small, so you will need a magnifying glass to see them. A good place to start

◄ This is a citrus fruit mite. Most plants and animals in your backyard will have populations of mites living on them.

looking for mites and other ectoparasites is on the soft bodies of snails and slugs. When you look through your magnifying glass, make sure you do not allow the Sun's rays to pass through, since they will burn the animal.

See if you find can find a caterpillar, a grasshopper, or an earthworm, and have a look at the ectoparasites they carry. If you have a net, try to catch a moth fluttering around an outside light at night. You will need to slip your animal into a jar while you look at it. Make sure you release the animal exactly where you found it afterward.

Plants, too, have lots of mites on them. Have a close look at leaves and fruits for these tiny **parasites.**

Books and websites

■ Downer, John. *Weird Nature.* Toronto: Firefly Books, 2002.

■ Knutson, Roger. *Fearsome Fauna.* New York: W. H. Freeman, 1999.

■ *Fun with worms and other minibeasts at* http://yucky.kids.discovery.com/flash/index.html

■ *Find out about parasites at* http://www.pbs.org/wgbh/nova/odyssey/hotscience.html

30

Words to Know

absorb
To draw digested food through the gut wall

alga
Plantlike single-celled organism (plural: algae)

bacteria
Very small single-celled organisms

blood vessel
Narrow tube through which blood flows

chlorophyll
Green pigment in plants that traps the energy of the Sun

chloroplast
Part of a plant that produces sugars

cellulose
Substance from which plant cell walls are made

commensalism
Relationship between two creatures in which one benefits but the other is unaffected

digest
To break down food in the gut so nutrients can be taken into the body

ectoparasite
Parasite that feeds on or through its host's skin

endoparasite
Parasite that lives inside its host's body

enzyme
Substance in the body that allows chemical reactions to occur

fungus
Plantlike organism; mushrooms are an example (plural: fungi)

host
Animal or plant that supports a parasite or commensal organism

larva
Young of an insect such as a fly (plural: larvae)

mucus
Thick, slimy fluid

mutualism
Relationship between two creatures in which both partners benefit

nectar
Sugary liquid produced by plants to reward pollinators

organism
Any living thing, including plants, animals, bacteria, fungi, and protists

parasite
Organism that benefits at the expense of another

protist
Animal- or plantlike single-celled organism

red blood cell
Blood cell that carries oxygen around the body

symbiosis
Close relationship between different types of creatures (plural: symbioses)

white blood cell
Blood cell that destroys invading organisms

Index

Numbers in *italics* refer to pictures.

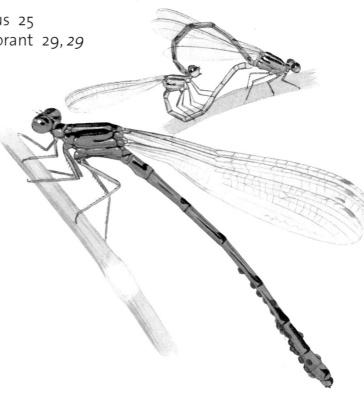